CAPISOGENEROSPECILISM

And the Plight of the Poor,

A Treatise

CHARLES MWEWA

Published by:
ACP
Ottawa, ON Canada
www.acpress.ca
www.springopus.com
Email:
info@acpress.ca

ISBN: 978-1-998788-87-3

DEDICATION

For

thought-leaders

across the globe – let us think our world
towards humane resource management.

CONTENTS

In this treatise, you will learn about:

- The novice concept of Capisogenerospecilism
- The conceptual frameworks in which the rich and poor are configured
- The limitations of both Capitalism and Socialism
- And the exemplification of the Capisogenerospecilistic Model

Capisogenerospecilism is, arguably, the best approach to the governance of the scarce resources in the developing countries. And it will also be the most coveted model in the developed countries in years to come. Countries and governments can no longer afford the luxuries of affordability leaning heavily towards the haves, leaving many people in a shambles, need or misery. A humane approach to ending poverty is, therefore, through the management of resources humanely and caringly, both for now and in the future. The plight of the poor must be the most important priority of governing, and one of the highest motivating forces in people.

Capisogenerospecilism is, therefore, an ideological framework that brings together relevant aspects of rich and poor thinkings discussed in this book, to solve human economic and social problems. It is a pragmatic model imbued in an ideological garb relevant to both governance and economic policy.

CAPISOGENEROSPECILISM

Three Schools of Thought

The following are the proposed three schools of thought that have formed the basis of worldviews on the governance of economic interests in many countries of the world:

1. The poor are made; therefore, their plight is society's doing or making
2. The poor are born; therefore, their plight is their own doing or making
3. The poor are neither born nor made; therefore, their plight is their own thinking

The Poor are Made Model

Society is a stratosphere of the poor and the rich. It might even seem obvious that society is designed to be a system comprising the poor and the rich. Everything in society points to this reality. Thus, many people still accept their statuses in society as socially constructed. In other words, some people think that society has defined them as poor or rich and as such that they have little or no power to change their statuses except with society's will. As society defines and regulates them, so they remain.

The rich do everything they can to be and remain rich and the poor are powerless to change their social standing. Government sets the social *agenda* and with the help of the poor, this *agenda* is meant to benefit and keep the rich and the poor where they are. For example, slaves, servants and peasants are fixed by social rules and regulations, and they cannot change that status, and are, therefore, condemned to live in poverty from generation to generation. They have come to relegate themselves, and do, in fact, accept their poor conditions and positions as norms. The rich and powerful, on the other hand, have solidified their position of power and privilege, and they continue to get richer and richer at the expense of the poor.

Thus, in certain societies, classes still exist. The power or upper class, the barely-making-it middle class and the struggling lower class. Each respective class must remain where it is and must be comfortable. The poor cheerlead the rich, and the rich expect to be endeared, served and worshipped by the poor. Change of poverty conditions depends on political and social policy, usually, set or designed by the aristocracy in olden days, and the upper class in contemporary times.

The Poor are Born Model

Some people think that they were born poor. They believe that they are fixed, and have no option for change. So, they relegate themselves to their poor statuses and are resigned to where they are. Poverty, to this school of thought, is inborn and innate. The system is set or designed in such a way that where one is born, automatically, defines and determines their status in life. And no matter what they do, the poor cannot become rich. And the rich are fixed where they are; they can only continue to be rich. Social and political policy favor them, because, in many ways, they set, design and help to shape public policy.

Neither Born Poor nor Made Model

This is a nature-nurture symbioticism. Poverty is seen, thus, to be neither a natural or social construct. The poor can change. The rich can be demoted. Thinking, ambition, and diligence, and some stroke of luck, have everything to do with where one is on the rich-poor continuum.

In this worldview, there are people who may have been born poor, but they rise above their condition of birth and become rich and well-to-do. Their thinking instructs them of who they are, and not social rules and political policy. They can navigate the world of business, education and set personal goals and redefined themselves. They are not contained in, or confined to, the sacks of servitude or political serfdom. They are free to change their statuses at will – through hard work, connections, determination or diligence.

Similarly, the rich can fall. They can fall when financial or other economic conditions are met (such as recession, inflation, divorce, sickness, loss of employment, death, etc.). They have no permanency bragging rights. Many, may be enjoying their wealth statuses on a leash. Survival is of the fittest, and birth has nothing to do with their wealth and power. They can choose to expend their wealth and power anyhow they please, and are free to made any changes they may desire.

Nature of Poverty

Poverty is Lack of Resources

In this view, to be poor is to have no resources or access to resources. Resources themselves can be in terms of human, capital, labor, land, raw materials, or technology. The difference between the rich and the poor is the presence of resources and access to them of one party, namely, the rich, and the lack of the same to the other, namely, the poor. The poor lack resources, and so, they are unable to meet their basic means of survival. This may lead them to lack housing, food and clean water. They need these things, but they are powerless to access them. And since money is the means of exchange, they lack money so that they are unable to exchange it for the things that they need.

The rich have the means, the access and the resources they need, and, therefore, they are able to enjoy their excesses as luxury and meet their wants. The rich are also likely to have money, and a lot of it, which ultimately give them an advantage in exchanging it with what they want. So, they can trade, buy what they need and want and have excess to spoiling their wanton demands.

Poverty is Not Desirable

Drawing from the above, poverty cannot be said to be desirable, because by nature, it impoverishes them and impedes on the people's physical, psychic or mental or social survival. The poor struggle to exist. They are unable to live as they wish. They are prone more to incurable diseases than the rich, and they cannot afford a basic survival kit (food, clean water and housing) of life.

Thus, the poor may, comparatively, live shorter lives, be uneducated, lack sophistication, and struggle to earn an income or make ends meet. The result is that they are subjected to servitude to survive. They must serve the rich, at the rich's dictation, to be able to fend a living in life. The poor are likely to be in bondage, destitution, and are invisible. They may have ideas, but these, if discovered, end up benefiting the rich. The poor are not free. They may not even be free to think properly, because their thought is distorted by need and lack of power.

People Try to Escape Poverty

All the efforts the poor make is an attempt at escaping poverty. Their efforts may look insignificant or even mundane, but they are meant to find a permanent solution to their poor quagmire. The poor aspire to be rich, and even for richness. That is why they endure and, in the process, fail to achieve their aspiration.

The rich aspire to ascend to the level where they can stop worrying about money and any other means to wealth. They want to build money empires which should outlive them, whether they have progeny or not. Because there is an implied reality that poverty brings shame in life and in death. Poverty erodes dignity and respect, and it socially excludes the poor from full participation in the economic, and the marketplace of ideas. The poor can vote, only to enhance the chances and prestiges of the rich. They can trade, only to put money into the pockets of the rich. They can work, only to earn disproportionately to the amount of time, energy and hard work they put into their work. They can be creative, only to ingratiate to the tastes and cravings of the rich. People normally do everything and can do anything to escape poverty until they fail and then accept or relegate themselves to a life of poverty and misery. In short, poverty breeds hopelessness.

Inevitability of Poverty

Poverty is inevitable. Even God has endorsed that prerogative: "The poor you will always have with you."[1] It is one of the most unpalatable statements, but also one of the most instructive. There are three reasons why every government and nation must prioritize the plight of the poor. The poor will always be there; they

---

[1] Mark 14:7

will always have expectations; and they are weak.

The poor will always be there

The poor will always be there. So, there is no guesswork. Government policy must prioritize the plight of the poor. This is not an after-thought action, it must be at the center of policy formulation and implementation. Because the poor will always be there, efforts must be made and rules be set to tackle poverty even before it manifests. More efforts must be made to prevent it. And even more efforts made to deal with it.

The poor have expectations

The poor expect to be rich or to be helped. This is a conundrum that escapes even the wit of the most talented. When we see the poor, the first thought that comes to our minds is, *they are lazy, why are they poorly dressed, why do they have malnutrition or why are they begging for bread?* We tend to forget or become negligent in our perspectives of what the poor think or go through.

The poor are hopeless. They are not in that position by choice, most of the time. They might have been brought to where they are by circumstances beyond their control. Therefore, the most injurious form of atrocity and oppression is that which neglects the plight of the poor, at individual or national level.

We do have justifications, all of us. When we see children begging for cents, shillings or *ngwees* on the street, or when a poor person approaches us for alms, or when they are willing to do the most menial jobs for us, our first reaction is that we despise them. We look down upon them. We advance assumptions such as, "These people are shameless," "They are wasteful," "They are a nuisance," "They must work hard," "They misspend what they get," "They lack accountability," etc. This is a misunderstanding, and it is only countenanced to justify our own sense of greed and lack of care. The poor are not capable even of changing their poverty conditions even remotely, of course, without external, non-governmental or even governmental help. They cannot escape a life of poverty once in it, at least, for or by themselves. They need help, genuine help.

That help may have something to do with the mindset of the poor or their belief system or even their tendency to wastefulness. These are tendencies the rich abhor and find unpalatable. Yet, the poor are hopeless and cannot change without help from the rich. In every nation, there is government, whether dictatorial or democratic, it is government nevertheless. Government must prioritize the plight of the poor, their state of mind and their physical wellbeing. And this must be an ongoing, infinite process. There can never be a time when government should say, "We have done enough."

Poverty reduces people to brainlessness. In short, they stop to think properly. The wealthy and the well-to-do must think for the poor. They must have compassion and treat the poor with understanding. When the poor are out of the jaws of poverty, they will remember.

Giving to the poor is not a waste, no matter how insignificant it might look. Matter of factly, the poor may not give back. And this is a discrepancy that demoralizes many people and prevents them from giving to the poor. They would rather give to those who will give them back in return. But each gift given to the poor is a mark of care, compassion and altruism. It counts to one's sense of gratitude that they are not themselves in the place of life.

Giving to the poor is one of the best ways of management of one's resources. When government sets up poverty alleviation schemes, it is investing well in its people. When individuals remember and give to the poor, they are accounting well for all the things they have and have received in life. The plight of the poor must be the priority of the rich.

The poor are weak

Poverty is a weakness; it is not a strength. The poor are inherently weak – they cannot do even the easiest things the rich find mundane and unchallenging. This is the thinking most people do not have. When a rich child looks at the map of the world, they see vacation destinations. When a poor child looks at the map of the world, he does not see himself in it, and in many cases, he may not even have a map to look at. When a rich girl watches

TV, she may aspire to be the one being broadcasted in future. But when a poor child looks at a TV set, she sees only colors and letters, and may not even have a TV set, in the first place.

The poor are too weak to speak, to challenge negativity and evil and to assert themselves as human beings. They are weak to even express their opinions. They die without any recognition. They do not see the world the way the rich do. To the poor, the entire world is a prison, a vindictive transaction, a blook of thorns and briars, and a whip to break their backs.

To many poor people, life is meaningless and death may even be desirable. They may have no goals, no plans, no frame of reference, and no hope. They are too weak to fight for their rights, and too weak to defend their humanity. Someone must always take their place and fight for them.

Belief, Myth, Assumption of Poverty

With poverty, there is a belief that it perpetuates itself. And to some extent, this belief holds. The phrase, the "rich get richer, and the poor, poorer," was framed from this belief. This is, experientially, that those who are rich continue to use (and sometimes, abuse) the poor, and, thus, relegating the poor to perpetual poverty.

There is a myth that poverty is a curse or a spirit. One does not need to be religious to entertain this myth. However, in the positive, it tends to highlight the very unpalatable fact that poverty is undesirable. It also solidifies the first idea we discussed that poverty is here to stay. However, preemptively, the myth or the intent to spiritualize poverty comes from the premise that people understand, implicitly, that poverty is bad and that they cannot do anything about it. This myth brings false peace to humanity and tends to justify the need to hold on to one's resources and not to share with the poor.

There is an informed assumption that poverty can only be reduced but cannot be permanently eradicated. And prior efforts have tended to prove this assumption right. However, it is also this assumption that has led to people and governments to give only lip-service to the fight against poverty and the plight of the poor. Even well-intentioned people and governments have placed little or only lackadaisical attitude towards the fight against poverty. In fact, and, ironically, most efforts to end or reduce poverty, end up enriching the very people who are already rich.

Dominance over Scarce Resources

As the earth's population increases, its resources decrease. So, there is, as expected, competition for the scarce resources. Those who may – through circumstance, chance or even industry - accumulate a lot of it or have advantage of more resources than others, are called rich. And those who do not have such advantages are called poor. As such, the rich will always dominate the poor.

There are three rules (laws) in nature that tend to favor selfish accumulation and manipulation of resources. These are: The more people have, the less they share; the more people lack, the less they will save; and people, generally, fear to repeat failure.

The more people have, the less they share

The more people have, the less they share. It is a rule of nature, a very cruel rule. People often misunderstand this rule; they presume that the more people have, the more they will share. Human instinct errs on the side of plenty, and more of it. Thus, once someone begins to accumulate, they continue to accumulate, even to the point of losing the meaning of accumulation.

And this is the foundation for greed and poverty. There are those who take this rule and manipulate it to their advantage. They may advance social and economic theories that favor this rule, too. To some extent, Capitalism is based on this rule. And the argument often made is that people must have freedom of contract, freedom of trade, freedom of property ownership and the equalization of opportunities but not of results.

These so-called lofty ideas are redundant. They are redundant because society is already stratified. From when people are born, they are already conscious of this reality. Children learn how not to share without any input from their parents. Each baby desires only to have and to hold, and nothing for sharing. Sharing is, therefore, not innate to humanity; it must be learned.

Society, families and governments must inculcate good sharing attitudes in children from early on. Without any such inculcation, people will default towards greed and self-aggrandizement. They will pursue any chance or avenue that lends itself to self-accumulation at the expense of sharing. Sometimes, humans hold on to things which will not even benefit them. They can have so much that it becomes meaningless, and yet, they will still not share unless they have been schooled into the intricacies of empathy, sympathy and compassion. To learn how to share, and to, in fact, share, is a genuine human achievement.

Therefore, those who presume that they will share only when they have more, are mistaken. The more they will have, the greedier they will become. If one cannot give in little, they will not give at all in much. Poverty emanates from such – because each one wants to have more and are not willing to share.

Socialism is not the opposite of Capitalism; it is an antithesis. It simply contradicts Capitalism. In Socialism, there is an assumption of common ownership, mostly, of the means of production (land, capital, labor, technology, etc.). Common ownership is not the same as sharing. And the experimental Eastern European Socialism has shown that discrepancy and weakness. When people claim to own something in common, they still form a small enclave of the so-called "owners" who tyrannize the majority. The few, actually, get so greedy that they exclude the majority, in the end, the system tends to create a servitude structure in which a few benefits enormously on the sweat of the majority. So, Socialism is a tragic exemplification of the sharing model. The concept of Capisogenerospecilism comes very close to the sharing model that could, if properly implemented, even end poverty in some respects.

The more people lack, the less they will save

The first is just like the second. Assumptively, people think that if they lack something, their immediate action when they have it, is that they will save. But reality speaks a different language. In fact, people do the opposite; they save more the more they have, and less the less they have. And foundationally, this does not, ironically, only inform poverty, but it perpetuates it as well.

Poverty, thus, self-perpetuates, and the experience of many people is that the poorer they are, the poorer they remain. And this, too, explains generational poverty and richness. As they say, the *have-nots* die without having and the *haves* live having more.

It takes a deliberate change of thinking, a sort of reversal of faculty structures to defeat generational poverty. Someone must be willing to break the cycle. In many cases, the one who does so may even die poor but leave behind an incredible structure that would sustain future generations into richness. The one who begins the saving process is the catalyst for generational wellness and wellbeing. This is because richness is the frugal transaction of scarce resources and the manipulation of the same towards long-term sustainability. People die, however rich they may be. The only true legacy they can, eventually, leave behind, is a reprogrammable thought pattern of savings and investments. That is how generational, and even, national poverty is broken. Disregard for this, lands peoples and nations into deep poverty and indebtedness.

People, generally, fear to repeat failure

This is a double-edged sword. In one sense it is good, because people do not want to fail twice or multiple times. But this, is also a cause of massive disparities between the *haves* and the *have-nots*. Those who emerge from poverty, may likely forget that they once were poor and keep everything to themselves. Those who are rich are sometimes oblivious to the plight of the poor for the same reason.

That innate fear of failure keeps them greedy. They fear that if they give or share, they will lose and become like the poor.

They have a point, but a misguided one. And this is one of the reasons why the rich give, *per capita*, less than the poor do. In national parlance, the trend is the manifestation of a shrinking number of billionaires and an expansive number of the poor. In some situations, one percent of the population may own ninety-nine percent of the resources. This is a gross misdirection of all that make humans, human. It is a gross disservice to nature, to God and to the best of human angels. But that is the reality, and more and more nations are trending towards that grossity (being grossly unjust).

However, redistribution is not the answer, either. In the vetted productivity cycle, distribution is, ultimately, the very end product of acquisition, production and investment. It is not the beginning. To redistribute, therefore, is to, unfairly, impinge upon others' sacrifices, creativity and resourcefulness. It is theft of hefty proportions. Others cannot work very hard only to dump it into the hands of the lazy.

The people may hope that those who have accumulated should redistribute their fortunes and equalize. Even divine law does not advocate for equalization of fortunes. Those who have more, will have more. Those who do not have or did not utilize their brain power, wisdom, energy, time and opportunities to have more, will lose everything.

This is a salience that is entertained by all the major religious and philosophical leanings. And there is some justification to that. People should earn their pay. The best the poor can do is to work for their wages, and from then, aim to become their own bosses. That is a humane form of sharing.

The rich have a role to play to end or alleviate poverty conditions in the world. They should not give away their resources, for they, in most cases, have worked very hard to manage it. But they can create labor and provide avenues for employing those who are willing and are qualified to work.

Government, too, has a role to play to end or alleviate poverty; government can create legislation that provides conducive and an enabling environment for people to trade, conduct business and enter into contracts without duress, corruption or unfair practices.

This will empower both the *haves* and the *have-nots*, and the end product is a sharing of responsibilities towards a harmonious and wealth society. The poor, too, have a role to play; they should be *willing* to work as long as such work respects their human rights, and does not subject them to slavery conditions of labor.

Conceptual Capisogenerospecilism

Either rich or poor

The thinking that one can either be rich or poor, and that there is no middle ground, is a central weakness of the indomitable western and the adopted modern economic theorization. And the major weakness of Captalism, too. By embracing this thinking, conscience is forfeited, giving way to uncommon greed and selfishness. People should have the right to own all the means of production but doing so humanely, and, where it is possibly, equitably.

Neither rich nor poor

The inability to accept that one can neither be rich nor poor, and that they will always resort to the either-or paradigm, has messed up public economic and global policy. The goal of public policy is to build a society that strives to eliminate poverty across sectorial spheres. The neither rich nor poor thinking cannot be allowed to exist in that arrangement. The saying, "make me neither rich nor poor," is a wise adage affixed to the requirement to obfuscate one's avaricious instincts in preference for the prevailing and unfair hardliner obsequiousness.

There is no society that is neither rich nor poor, serve for a utopic fig of imagination. Wherever people are, there are rich one and poor ones. This is how it has always been.

Therefore, only a combination of regulation of excesses through graduated taxation, for example, and competition, and the deregulation of enterprise where feasible, lend a key factorial consideration towards a more balanced society. The rich must not be disbarred because they are rich, and the poor must not be penalized for being poor. A people with an active conscience and a government with reason must appreciate these factors and account for their derogation or facilitation.

From the General to the Specific

This is the policy of targeting the wellbeing of the general population to meeting the needs of an individual. The entire premise of Socialism rests on this theoretical framework. However, what it has produced has been the *tyranny of a minority* and the manipulation and abuse of people's labor and capital rights. The other framework below, has not worked satisfactorily and well, either.

From the Specific to the General

This is the policy of empowering specific individuals to ignite a general good. This framework looks and sounds humane in the interim, but it has tended to produce a society that is imbued in corruption and avaricious acts of graft, misappropriation and greed.

This was the province of Capitalism all along. What it has, however, done is to create a society of the extreme *haves* and *have-nots*, a society so full of disparities that others are dying with hunger when others are throwing food away. This framework is fundamentally flawed, wrong and unfair. It creates a dual citizenry of need and bounty. In the long run, it fails to create balance, leading to a gaping chasm between the rich and the poor.

The Remarkability of Capisogenerospecilism

Capisogenerospecilism is an ideological framework that brings together relevant aspects of the above frameworks to solve human economic problems. It is a pragmatic model imbued in an ideological garb relevant to both governance and economic policy. It frees governments to regulate or deregulate according to need, in the best interest of human good. This will bring balance and end inequalities, and in the long term, solve the persistent problem of poverty.

Salient Features of Capisogenerospecilism

Panacea to the deficiencies of historical Capitalism and Socialism

Unlike pure Capitalism or Socialism, Capisogenerospecilism provides a balance between personal freedoms and social good. This must lead to social wellbeing of individuals and citizens.

Compensability of labor

Capisogenerospecilism asserts that labor must be compensated, because it is an exchange of time, energy and force exerted. No-one should work for nothing unless it is a gratuity. And no matter how low or menial their work, people must be respected and treated fairly. Wages, too, must be legislated so people can exercise their rights to collective bargaining or unionization. Labor laws must be in place to guarantee fundamental labor rights and the suitability of working conditions to the plight of all concerned.

Capitalization of capital

Almighty capital must be capitalized and underlined. Society must respond to inherent human entrepreneurial leaning. Government and lending institutions and fiscal policies must be streamlined to target small and medium enterprises. And people must have the right to access capital freely, respectably, and without discrimination.

Land must be landed

Land is the property of every citizen held in trust for them by the governors. It is not subject to arbitrary transaction or allocation except with the consent of the governed. Thus, every citizen must have a right to accessible and reasonably priced land.

Land must be deregulated or minimally regulated, and for the purposes of housing and farming, land must be available to everyone who can utilize it. The concept of "Citizen First," must be implemented to secure land, first for the citizen and last for the foreigner. This approach must be constitutionalized to guarantee citizens' land ownership rights.

Primacy of technology

Government must invest heavily in technology for the sole benefit of its citizens. Every inch of innovation and experimentation must be explored to provide workable and accessible technologies to the people, starting from kindergarten.

Moreover, educational institutions must be encouraged to be innovative in scope, and incentives must be provided to encourage boys and girls to elect sciences, mathematics and technology. And where possible, technological subjects must be made compulsory for all students. This model does not impale artistry, it only supplements it.

Capisogenerospecilism and Governance: Conclusion

The key thrust and summary of Capisogenerospecilism is contained into this maxim, "The need of one, the need for us all." This, too, is a principled approach to governance. Government must be the institutionalization of need. And this is established by five tenets:

1. Humane approach to human needs;
2. Celebration of the process and sharing of benefits as the end product;
3. The enrichment of all is a goal, fulfilling one need at a time;
4. The policy of targeting one, because it is one that makes all;
5. And all are important because no-one is unimportant.

The five tenets, collectively, establish the ethical and practical approach to the management of resources to and for the benefit of all.

Thus, Capisogenerospecilism creates a paradigm shift from the business and transactional approach to the humane approach; from the celebration of results only to one of celebrating the process as well; from the enrichment of one, to the enrichment of all; from the global targeting approach to one that targets one individual to benefit all; and finally, from making specific individuals, such as leaders or rich people or the president important, to the making of all important at the expense of none.

ABOUT THE AUTHOR

Award-Winning, Best-Selling Author,
Charles Mwewa (LLB; BA Law; BA Ed;
LLM), is a prolific researcher, poet, novelist,
lawyer, law professor and Christian apologist
and intercessor. Mwewa has written no less
than 100 books and counting in every genre
and has exhibited his works at prestigious
expos like the Ottawa International Book
Expo and is the winner of the Coppa Awards
for his signature publication, *Zambia: Struggles of
My People.*
Mwewa and his family live in the Canadian
Capital City of Ottawa.

SELECTED BOOKS BY THIS AUTHOR

1. *ZAMBIA: Struggles of My People (First and Second Editions)*
2. *10 FINANCIAL & WEALTH ATTITUDES TO AVOID*
3. *10 STRATEGIES TO DEFEAT STRESS AND DEPRESSION: Creating an Internal Safeguard against Stress and Depression*
4. *100+ REASONS TO READ BOOKS*
5. *A CASE FOR AFRICA?S LIBERTY: The Synergistic Transformation of Africa and the West into First-World Partnerships*
6. *DECOLONIZATION: Reclaiming African Originality and Destiny*
7. *A PANDEMIC POETRY, COVID-19*
8. *ALLERGIC TO CORRUPTION: The Legacy of President Michael Sata of Zambia*
9. *BOOK ABOUT SOMETHING: On Ultimate Purpose*
10. *CAMPAIGN FOR AFRICA: A Provocative Crusade for the Economic and Humanitarian Decolonization of Africa*
11. *CHAMPIONS: Application of Common Sense and Biblical Motifs to Succeed in Both*

Worlds

12. *FURGUSON FACTOR: Motivation, Strategy, Tactics*
13. *CORONAVIRUS PRAYERS*
14. *HH IS THE RIGHT MAN FOR ZAMBIA: And Other Acclaimed Articles on Zambia and Africa*
15. *I BOW: 3500 Prayer Lines of Inspiration & Intercession from the Heart: Volume One*
16. *INTERUNIVERSALISM IN A NUTSHELL: For Iranian Refugee Claimants*
17. *JURISPRUDENCE of GOOD AND RIGHT: A Treatise on Juridical Activism and Fiat*
18. *LAW & GRACE: An Expository Study in the Rudiments of Sin and Truth*
19. *LAWS OF INFLUENCE: 7even Lessons in Transformational Leadership*
20. *LOVE IDEAS IN COVID PANDEMIC TIMES: For Couples & Lovers*
21. *P.A.S.S: Version 2: Answer Bank*
22. *P.A.S.S.: Acing the Ontario Paralegal-Licensing Examination, Version 2*
23. *POETRY: The Best of Charles Mwewa*
24. *QUOT-EBOS: Essential. Barbs. Opinions. Sayings*

.

INDEX

www.ingramcontent.com/pod-product-compliance
Lightning Source LLC
Chambersburg PA
CBHW032306210326
41520CB00047B/2262